SUPER SIMPLE
SCIENCE AT WORK

SUPER SIMPLE
EXPERIMENTS
WITH
LIGHT AND COLOR

FUN AND INNOVATIVE SCIENCE PROJECTS

PAIGE V. POLINSKY

CONSULTING EDITOR, DIANE CRAIG, M.A./READING SPECIALIST

Super Sandcastle

An Imprint of Abdo Publishing
abdopublishing.com

abdopublishing.com

Published by Abdo Publishing, a division of ABDO, PO Box 398166, Minneapolis, Minnesota 55439. Copyright © 2017 by Abdo Consulting Group, Inc. International copyrights reserved in all countries. No part of this book may be reproduced in any form without written permission from the publisher. Super SandCastle™ is a trademark and logo of Abdo Publishing.

Printed in the United States of America, North Mankato, Minnesota
062016
092016

THIS BOOK CONTAINS
RECYCLED MATERIALS

Editor: Liz Salzmann
Content Developer: Nancy Tuminelly
Cover and Interior Design and Production: Mighty Media, Inc.
Photo Credits: Mighty Media, Inc.; Shutterstock

The following manufacturer/name appearing in this book is a trademark: Kleenex®

Library of Congress Cataloging-in-Publication Data

Names: Polinsky, Paige V., author.
Title: Super simple experiments with light and color : fun and innovative science projects / Paige V. Polinsky ; consulting editor, Diane Craig, M.A./reading specialist.
Description: Minneapolis, Minnesota : Abdo Publishing, [2017] | | Series: Super simple science at work
Identifiers: LCCN 2016006223 (print) | LCCN 2016013049 (ebook) | ISBN 9781680781717 (print) | ISBN 9781680776140 (ebook)
Subjects: LCSH: Light--Experiments--Juvenile literature. | Color--Experiments--Juvenile literature. | Science--Experiments--Juvenile literature. | Science projects--Juvenile literature.
Classification: LCC QC360 .P65 2016 (print) | LCC QC360 (ebook) | DDC 535.078--dc23
LC record available at http://lccn.loc.gov/2016006223

Super SandCastle™ books are created by a team of professional educators, reading specialists, and content developers around five essential components—phonemic awareness, phonics, vocabulary, text comprehension, and fluency—to assist young readers as they develop reading skills and strategies and increase their general knowledge. All books are written, reviewed, and leveled for guided reading and early reading intervention programs for use in shared, guided, and independent reading and writing activities to support a balanced approach to literacy instruction.

To Adult Helpers

The projects in this title are fun and simple. There are just a few things to remember to keep kids safe. Some projects require the use of sharp or hot objects. Also, kids may be using messy materials such as glue or paint. Make sure they protect their clothes and work surfaces. Review the projects before starting, and be ready to assist when necessary.

KEY SYMBOLS

Watch for these warning symbols in this book. Here is what they mean.

LASER!
You will be working with a laser pointer. Never shine it in your or someone else's eye. This could cause blindness!

SHARP!
You will be working with a sharp object. Get help!

CONTENTS

LIGHT
AT WORK

Think of all the things you see each day. You see other people, animals, trees, clouds, and more! Did you know you cannot see those things without light?

Light makes things visible. It is also what lets us see different colors. Most natural light comes from the sun. There is also artificial light, such as the light from a lamp.

LIGHT MAKES BUTTERFLIES VISIBLE.

AUTUMN COLORS IN SUNLIGHT

LIGHT ENERGY

Light is a type of energy. Light energy travels in waves. These waves are always moving. Waves of sunlight travel billions of miles. They **eventually** hit Earth. Then they are either **absorbed** or reflected by objects.

COLOR

Light from the sun is called white light. But it is not white! It is actually made up of seven colors. They are red, orange, yellow, green, blue, indigo, and violet.

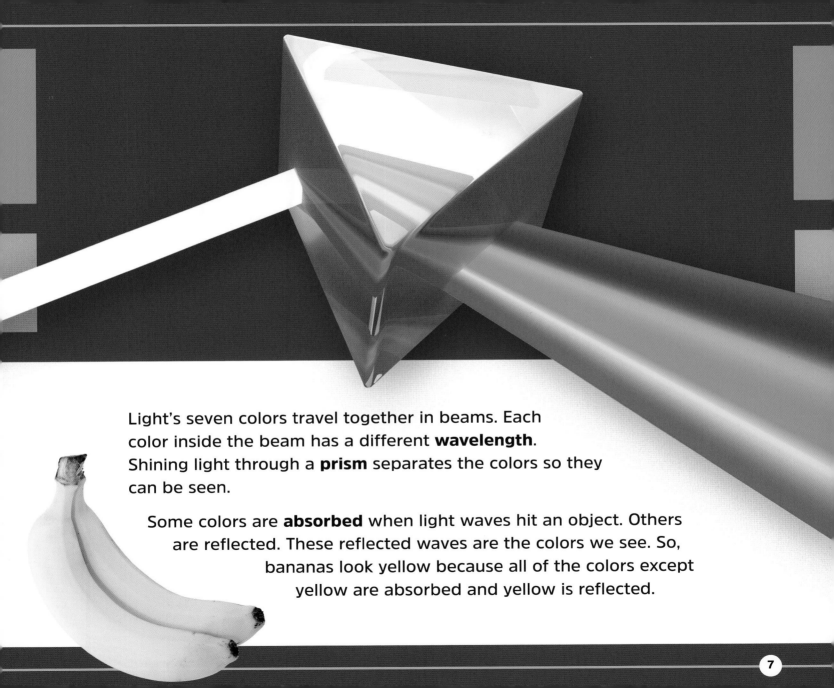

Light's seven colors travel together in beams. Each color inside the beam has a different **wavelength**. Shining light through a **prism** separates the colors so they can be seen.

Some colors are **absorbed** when light waves hit an object. Others are reflected. These reflected waves are the colors we see. So, bananas look yellow because all of the colors except yellow are absorbed and yellow is reflected.

WORK LIKE
A SCIENTIST

You've learned about light and color. Now you're ready to experiment! Scientists have a special way of working. It is called the Scientific Method. Follow the steps to work like a scientist. It's super simple!

THE SCIENTIFIC METHOD

Have a notebook and pencil handy. Scientists write down everything that happens in their experiments. They also write down their thoughts and ideas.

1. QUESTION

What question are you trying to answer? Write down your question. Then do some **research** to find out more about it.

2. GUESS

Try to guess the answer to your question. Write down your guess.

ALBERT EINSTEIN

Albert Einstein was a scientist. He came up with new ideas about space and time. Einstein was working in a patent office in 1905. That year, he wrote several important papers. One was on a new **theory** of light. He said light was made up of **particles** instead of continuous waves. His theories were later proven to be true!

3. EXPERIMENT

Create an experiment to help answer your question. Write down the steps. Make a list of the supplies you'll need. Then do the experiment. Write down what happens.

4. ANALYSIS

Study the results of your experiment. Did it answer your question? Was your guess correct?

5. CONCLUSION

Think about how the experiment went. Why was your guess wrong or right? Write down the reasons.

MATERIALS

Here are some of the materials that you will need for the experiments in this book.

CDs

CLEAR GLASS ORNAMENT

COLORED CELLOPHANE

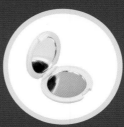

COMPACT MIRROR

DINNER KNIFE

DUCT TAPE

FLASHLIGHT

INDEX CARDS

JELLY BEANS

LASER POINTER

MARKERS

MODELING CLAY

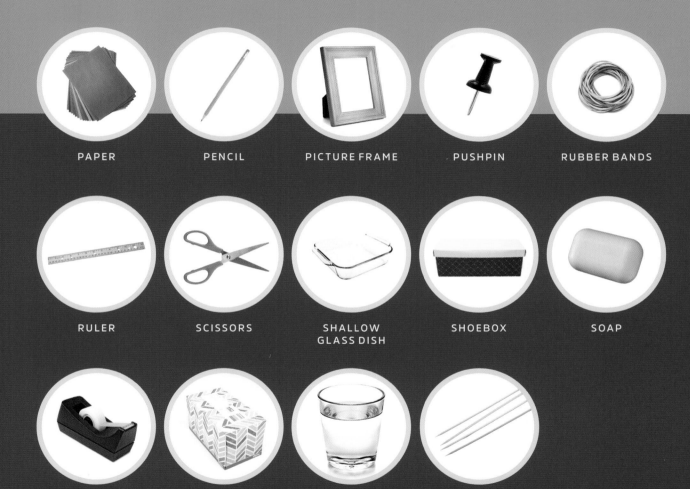

PAPER

PENCIL

PICTURE FRAME

PUSHPIN

RUBBER BANDS

RULER

SCISSORS

SHALLOW
GLASS DISH

SHOEBOX

SOAP

TAPE

TISSUE BOX

WATER

WOODEN SKEWERS

LIGHT-BEAM RELAY

Light travels in waves. These tiny waves move up and down. They are too small for us to see. But these waves also move forward all together. That is why we see light move forward in a straight line.

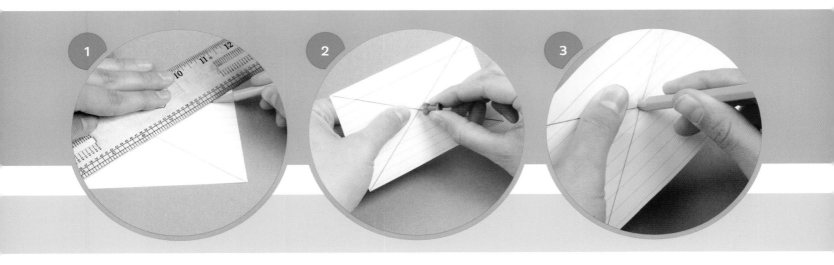

LEARN HOW LIGHT BEAMS TRAVEL!

1 Use the ruler and pencil to draw an X on each index card.

2 Use the pushpin to make a hole in the center of each X.

3 Use a sharpened pencil to make the pushpin holes bigger.

4 Place a small rectangle of clay on a long edge of each index card.

5 Stick the cards upright along the edge of a piece of paper. Each card should form a T shape with the paper.

Continued on the next page.

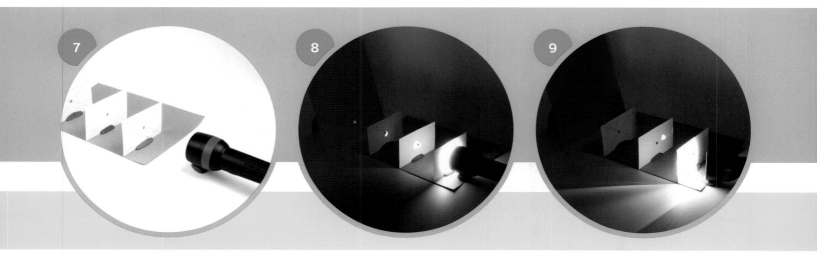

LIGHT-BEAM RELAY (CONTINUED)

⑥ Tape a piece of paper to the front of the picture frame. Set the frame at one end of the paper.

⑦ Set the flashlight at the end opposite the frame. Use clay to raise the flashlight. It should shine directly on the holes.

⑧ Turn off the lights and turn on the flashlight. Do you see a spot of light on the paper?

⑨ Angle the flashlight slightly so it does not shine directly at the holes. Is there still a spot of light on the paper?

WHY IT WORKS

Light travels in a straight line. The flashlight beam travels to the index cards. The first index card blocks or **absorbs** much of the light. Some of the straight beams travel through the punched holes. That is because the holes are lined up exactly. Moving the flashlight changes the result. The light beam points in another direction. It no longer lines up with the holes in the other index cards. So, it doesn't shine through to the paper at the end.

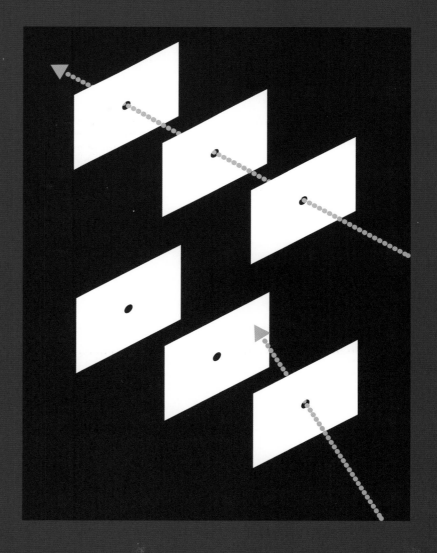

BENDING
LASER BEAMS

MATERIALS: shallow glass dish, water, dinner knife, bar of soap, laser pointer, clear glass ornament, compact mirror

Glass is **transparent**. Light travels through it. But the thickness and shape of glass can affect the way we see light. Use a mirror and a glass ornament to see how!

WHY IT WORKS

The laser beam appears to travel straight at first. But the glass dish actually makes the beam bend slightly. So does the water. Light bends anytime it travels through something different. The glass ornament bends the laser beam more. The mirror is also glass. But it is backed by a shiny surface that reflects light. This surface causes the beam to travel in a new direction.

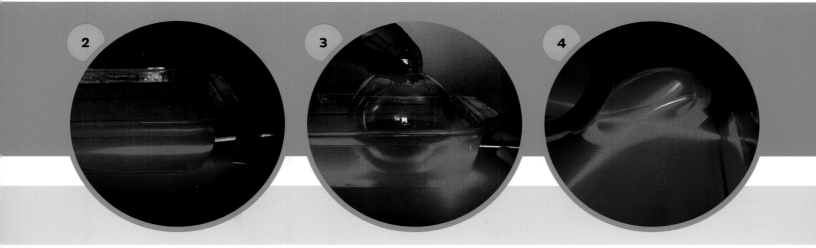

BEND LIGHT WITH GLASS!

① Fill the glass dish with water. Use the knife to scrape off a bit of soap. Stir the soap into the water until it **dissolves**.

② Turn off the lights. Shine the laser through the dish. You should see a straight light beam in the cloudy water.

③ Push the ornament into the water. Hold it in front of the light. What happens to the beam?

④ Remove the ornament. Place the mirror in the water. Hold it in front of the light. What happens to the beam?

FLASHLIGHT COLOR SHOW

MATERIALS: cellophane (red, green & blue), 3 flashlights, scissors, 3 rubber bands

Have you ever mixed paints together to create a new color? Maybe you mixed red and blue to make purple. You can create all kinds of colors by mixing colors together. This color creation occurs because paint **absorbs** colors. They become darker the more colors you mix together. Colors of light do just the opposite. They become brighter when you mix them!

MIX LIGHT TO CREATE COLORS!

① Fold a piece of colored cellophane in half.

② Wrap the cellophane around a flashlight lens. Secure it with a rubber band.

③ Repeat steps 1 and 2 with the other flashlights. Each flashlight should be wrapped in a different color of cellophane.

④ Turn off the lights. Shine the green and blue flashlights on a blank wall. Make their beams **overlap**. What color do they make?

Continued on the next page.

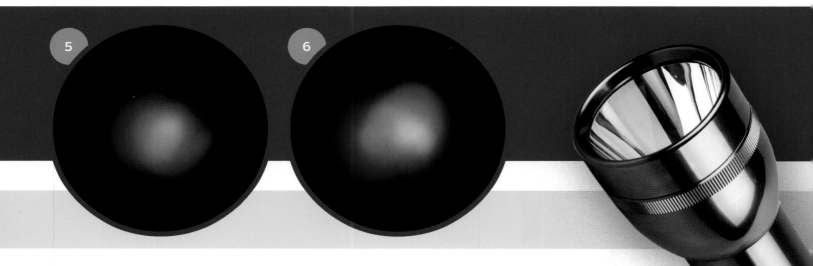

FLASHLIGHT COLOR SHOW (CONTINUED)

5 Shine the red and blue flashlights together. Then try mixing the red and green lights. Do they make different colors?

6 Have a friend help you combine all three colors. What happens?

WHY IT WORKS

Red, blue, and green are the primary colors of light. Each of these colors has a certain **wavelength**. These wavelengths interact in a way that makes us see different, brighter colors. Layering red and green produces yellow. Green and blue create **cyan**. Mixing red and blue makes magenta. And adding all three colors together creates white!

JELLY BEAN
JUMBLE

MATERIALS: shoebox, flashlight, pencil, scissors, ruler, jelly beans, cellophane (red, green & blue), rubber band

White light is not actually white. It is made up of seven colors. These colors move in waves. Each color has a different **wavelength**. Some wavelengths are **absorbed** when light hits an object. Others are reflected. The reflected wavelengths are the colors we see!

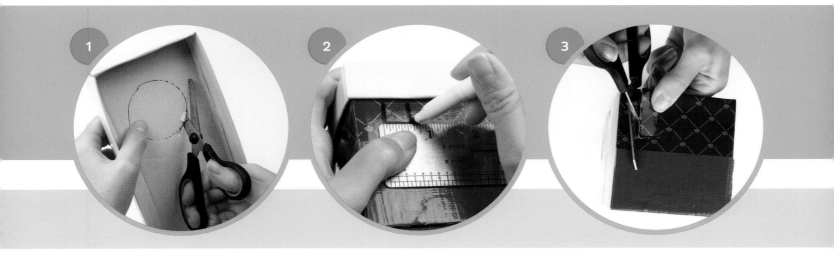

TURN JELLY BEANS DIFFERENT COLORS!

1 Stand the flashlight on one end of the shoebox lid. Trace the lens. Cut out the circle.

2 Place the lid on the shoe box. Draw a 1-inch (2.5 cm) square below the lid. Draw only three sides. The bottom of the shoe box lid will be one side of the square.

3 Remove the lid. Extend the sides of the square to the top of the box. Cut out the rectangle.

Continued on the next page.

JELLY BEAN JUMBLE (CONTINUED)

④ Put the jelly beans in the box. Put the lid on. The round hole should be opposite from the square hole.

⑤ Shine the flashlight into the round hole. Look at the jelly beans through the square hole.

⑥ Cover the flashlight with red cellophane. Secure it with a rubber band. Shine the flashlight into the hole. Do the jelly beans look different?

⑦ Cover the flashlight with blue cellophane. Then use green. What happens to the jelly bean colors?

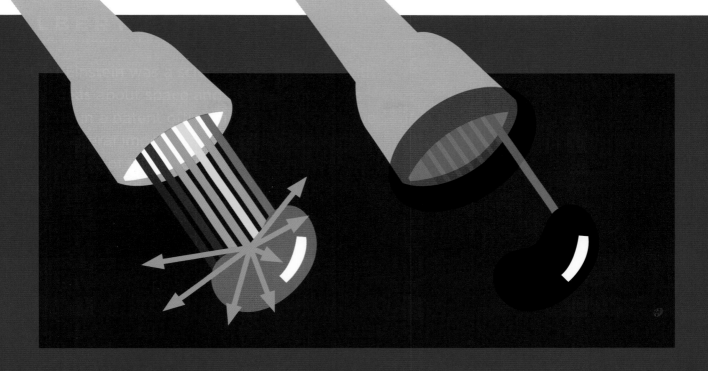

WHY IT WORKS

The flashlight produces white light. A green jelly bean in white light **absorbs** all colors except green. The green light waves reflect off the jelly bean. So the jelly bean looks green. But the red cellophane absorbs all colors from the light except red. Only red light waves come through. There is no green light to hit the green jelly bean. So it does not look green. It looks black! What other colors change in the red light? What about in the blue and green light?

BOX OF
RAINBOWS

MATERIALS: tissue box, scissors, 4 CDs, duct tape, flashlight

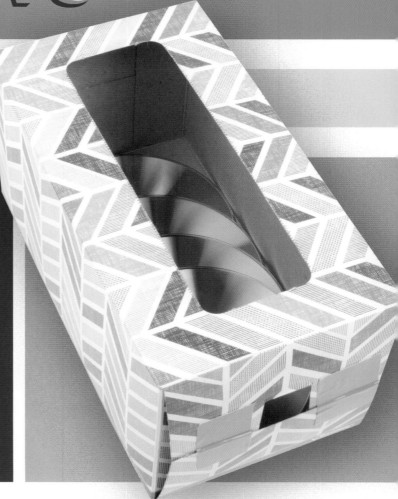

Rain showers can be **dreary**. But sometimes they make colorful rainbows appear! How does this happen? Sunlight passes through water droplets during a rain shower. The droplets are **prisms**. They make the sun's white light separate into its seven colors. We see red, orange, yellow, green, blue, indigo, and violet. Shining light on CDs can have a similar effect.

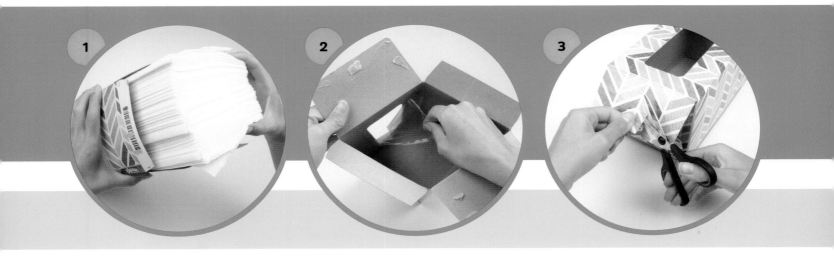

CREATE RAINBOWS IN A BOX!

① **Open one end of the box. If there are tissues inside, remove them.**

② **Remove the plastic lining from the top opening.**

③ **Cut a small square out of the top side flap. It should be just big enough to look through.**

Continued on the next page.

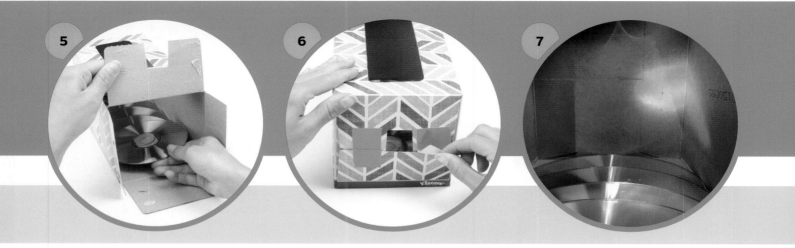

BOX OF RAINBOWS (CONTINUED)

④ Tape a CD to the bottom of the box. The shiny side should face up.

⑤ Repeat step 4 with the other CDs. The edge of each CD should cover the hole of the CD under it.

⑥ Tape the end of the box closed.

⑦ Shine the flashlight through the top of the box. Look through the hole in the end. What do you see?

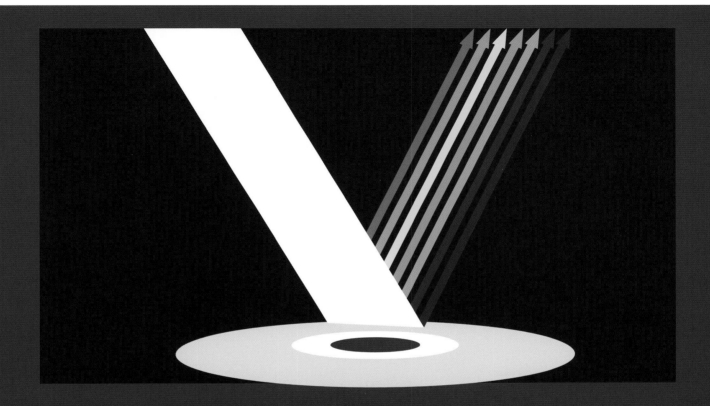

WHY IT WORKS

The surface of a CD is covered in tiny **ridges**. Light waves bounce off these ridges. The flashlight beam works like a ray of sunlight. It normally appears white. But the beam separates when it hits the CDs. The white light separates into colors. The separated colors are reflected onto the walls of the box. The ridges create a rainbow display for you to enjoy!

AFTERIMAGE SPIN

MATERIALS: 2 index cards, colored markers, duct tape, wooden skewer

Have you ever seen dark spots after a camera flash? Then you have experienced an afterimage! Your eyes and brain work together so you can see the world. Light travels to your eyes. Your eyes send messages to your brain. But they do not always work perfectly. Bright lights can make your eyes tired. This can cause you to see colors or images that do not exist!

WHY IT WORKS

Spinning the skewer spins the images. They flash back and forth very quickly. They move too fast for you to process! The skewer turns the card to side two. But your brain is still **reacting** to side one. And your brain is still processing side two when the card returns to side one. This causes you to combine the two images into a single picture!

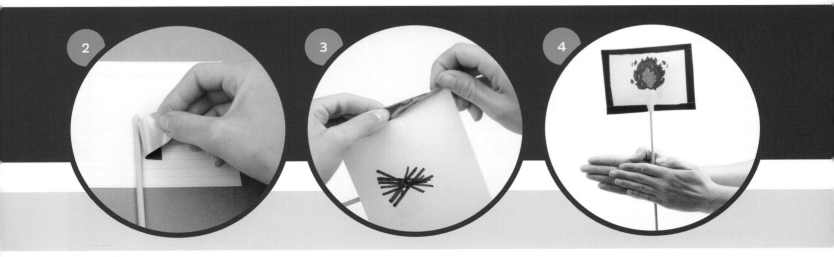

CREATE AN OPTICAL ILLUSION!

① Think of an image that has a top and a bottom. For example, a fire has both sticks and flames. Draw each part on a separate index card. Make sure the two parts line up.

② Tape the skewer to the back of one card.

③ Lay the other card on top of the first. The images should face out. Tape the cards' edges together.

④ Hold the skewer between your hands. Slide your hands back and forth. This makes the skewer spin. What do you see?

GLOSSARY

absorb – to soak up or take in.

dissolve – to become part of a liquid.

dreary – sad or gloomy.

eventually – in the end or at a later time.

overlap – to lie partly on top of something.

particle – a very small piece of matter, such as an atom or molecule.

prism – a transparent object that usually has three sides and bends light so that it separates into rainbow colors.

react – to move or behave in a certain way because of something else.

research – the act of finding out more about something.

ridge – a narrow, raised area on the surface of something.

theory – an idea that is the starting point for an argument or investigation.

transparent – clear or able to be seen through.

wavelength – the distance from the peak of one wave to the peak of the next wave.